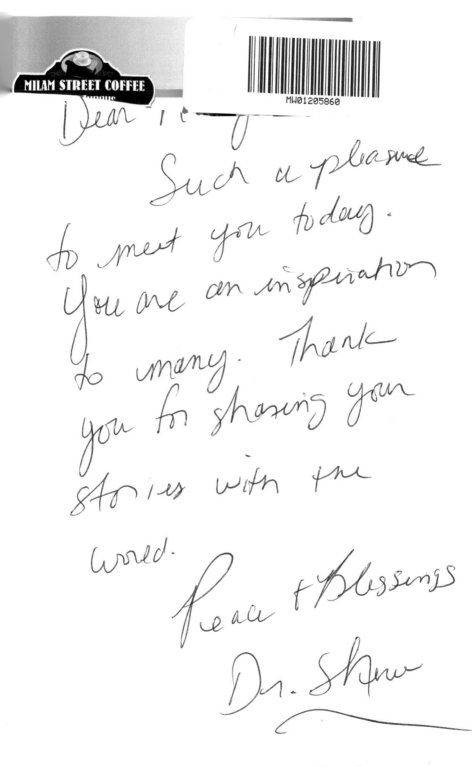

MILAM STREET COFFEE

MW01205860

Dear [...],

Such a pleasure
to meet you today.
You are an inspiration
to many. Thank
you for sharing your
stories with the
world.

Peace + Blessings

Dr. Shaw

3-2-19

WHAT A DIFFERENCE A
Change Makes!

21 Jewels of Wisdom for Living
Your Treasured Life

DR. SHEREE BRYANT SÉKOU

BALBOA.
PRESS
A DIVISION OF HAY HOUSE

Balboa Press books may be ordered through booksellers or by contacting:

Balboa Press
A Division of Hay House
1663 Liberty Drive
Bloomington, IN 47403
www.balboapress.com
1 (877) 407-4847

Because of the dynamic nature of the Internet, any web addresses or links contained in this book may have changed since publication and may no longer be valid. The views expressed in this work are solely those of the author and do not necessarily reflect the views of the publisher, and the publisher hereby disclaims any responsibility for them.

The author of this book does not dispense medical advice or prescribe the use of any technique as a form of treatment for physical, emotional, or medical problems without the advice of a physician, either directly or indirectly. The intent of the author is only to offer information of a general nature to help you in your quest for emotional and spiritual well-being. In the event you use any of the information in this book for yourself, which is your constitutional right, the author and the publisher assume no responsibility for your actions.

Any people depicted in stock imagery provided by Getty Images are models, and such images are being used for illustrative purposes only. Certain stock imagery © Getty Images.

Print information available on the last page.

ISBN: 978-1-9822-1010-6 (sc)
ISBN: 978-1-9822-1012-0 (hc)
ISBN: 978-1-9822-1011-3 (e)

Library of Congress Control Number: 2018909613

Balboa Press rev. date: 12/21/2018

NOTE FROM THE AUTHOR

I celebrate you and your choice to live differently. Because you don't pick up a book like this one unless you have chosen, consciously or subconsciously, to live differently. What I know now for sure is this: whenever I've decided to live differently, it has required change. I am not speaking of change merely for the sake of change. I am referring to change with purpose and meaning!

I realize change can be overwhelming, and this book is designed to reduce the overwhelm and support you along your change journey. We begin with an introduction so we can clarify positive change, talk through some of the fundamentals of change, and amplify the role the Soul plays in identifying and incorporating positive change into your life. We continue with twenty-one passages, each dedicated to a specific area of positive change. Each passage contains a simple, straight-forward message for your consideration, a memorable Jewel of Wisdom or key takeaway, and space for you to reflect on how to apply the passage to your life in a meaningful way. The book also includes quotes from leaders, teachers, and mentors whose words and work have helped change my life for the better. This book is small on purpose, so you can place it on your nightstand, meditation area, desk—wherever it can serve as a ready reference for inspiration and motivation on your journey. Feel free to read it cover to cover or take it in bit by bit, focusing on the areas you need most.

I have used the principles in the book to create positive changes in my professional and personal life, and I know you can too. I believe in your ability to be all you envision yourself to be. Allow the following passages and your powerful reflections to serve as a trusted companion on your change journey.

Wishing you peace, pleasure and a life you treasure...

In a situation where a discomfort or non-progressive attainment is being experienced, one must apply a change. For a change to be positive, it must be win-win, because the new situation *must not!* cannot be worse than the former situation that we already had. Positive change is hope for betterment.

— *Chief Dr. Ifagbenusola Olalekan Atanda*

INTRODUCTION

> We cannot become what we want
> by remaining what we are.
>
> –Max De Pree

Positive change is change with the explicit intention of making things better. Positive change implicitly trusts, acknowledges, and accepts the impact of Divine Order in harmony with responsibility, choice, and action. This book offers words of hope and inspiration from people I admire whose work has motivated me along my change journey and contains many of the tools and techniques I have used to change my life for the better. It also offers practical tools on how to create positive change, tips for taking personal responsibility for changing what you can, and reflections for you to commit to act in ways that work best for you.

In my work with individuals and organizations

all over the globe, managing change is a recurring theme and critical factor for success in business and in life. Change is the new black—it is everywhere we turn. I view embracing and navigating change as a superpower, one that contributes to inner peace, promotes self-actualization, and provides a positive contribution to our world. As leaders, we must lead ourselves first, and we must never underestimate the power of positive change.

Each time I have endeavored to improve my life, something had to change. I believe the same is true for you. Whether you are becoming an entrepreneur, advancing your side hustle, taking the "big leap" to pursue entrepreneurship full-time, looking for a better job, choosing to love yourself more, deciding to end relationships and begin again, something has got to change. For those of you who hold a powerful new and expansive vision for your life, your family, and your community: if what you have in mind is wildly different than what you currently experience, KNOW some things and sometimes someone must change. In my case that someone has often been me.

> True wisdom comes to each of
> us when we realize how little we
> understand about life, ourselves,
> and the world around us.
>
> –Socrates

My early efforts toward positive change were a lot like the typical "fight, flight or freeze" responses. I tried to fight the messages I was given that told me to terminate certain "good jobs" to pursue work more aligned with my strengths and calling. I tried to run away from toxic relationships and harmful situations, but I couldn't run far enough away to get them out of my head. At times I was stuck—allowing worry to consume me but not engaging in or committing to concrete action. When I got finally sick and tired, I went forward like a bullet! I committed to change, and I tried to change everything I could—all at the same time. I had great success, but my success came at a price. I got caught up in a cycle of chronic overdoing. **There was no balance in my approach to change.** I struggle to remember parts of my success because I was moving so fast, taking on entirely too much. I wanted it all and I wanted it now and I got it, or most of it. Somewhere along my journey I was doing what people said I should do, but I wasn't listening to myself or my body. My mind was telling me to take it easy. My body was telling me to slow down. But I don't think I really knew how. Today I realize I was unwilling to take a good look at my capacity because I didn't want to admit I had limits.

Still, I knew there had to be a better way. I began to seek out teachers and mentors who offered a more balanced approach to success. I started listening to audio books and podcasts while traveling to reframe my mindset and open myself to new ways of approaching business and life. I realized I was not alone on this journey, but I had to be willing to take steps to change things for the better in my life.

I didn't get a do-over, but I found ways do things differently. Today I boldly own my strengths and limitations, and I make far fewer apologies. I am gentler and more loving with myself —allowing more time to pray and pace myself along my journey towards positive change. There are still aspects of my work that are intense, but I have moved away from the violence of overdoing. Today I choose not to race or compete. I do not seek or expect perfection. Instead it is just me committing to doing my best and bringing my best to everything I do and everyone I encounter.

What I know for sure is this: bit by bit, you can change your life for the better. I offer you this work as your partner in positive change. May you be inspired to create positive change in your life, on your terms. May the passages of this book and every quote and reflection inspire hope and give you comfort along your change journey.

THE FUNDAMENTALS OF POSITIVE CHANGE

> I now let go of worn out things,
> worn out conditions, and worn
> out relationships. Divine Order is
> now established and maintained
> in me and in my world.
>
> –Catherine Ponder

UNDERSTANDING CHANGE

The only thing constant is change, and we human beings are creatures of habit. When change collides with our habits and comfort zones, there might be some tension and discomfort, so it helpful to get clear on a few fundamentals:

❖ We must accept the fundamental truth that change is inevitable.

❖ We must accept responsibility for changing things for the better in our lives.

❖ We must remain open to the beauty change has in store for us.

> When you live in complete acceptance of what is, that is the end of all drama in your life.
>
> –Eckhart Tolle

It is wise to deepen our understanding of change because understanding aids in acceptance of what is. When we fail to accept what is in front of us, we relinquish our power and responsibility to make things better. In this state of perceived powerlessness, we might even feel like a victim of our circumstances. However, when we can accept what is, then we can position ourselves to make conscious change. Conscious change isn't change for the sake of change. Conscious change involves deep feeling, awareness, and concerted action towards shifting our circumstances in a more positive direction. As with many of life's challenges, the quest to understand change can be elusive, so it is helpful to be aware of some of the causes of change. In my experience, change typically emerges in one of three ways (or a beautiful combination of the three):

1. CHANGE as CALLING: Change as Calling occurs when change is initiated specifically in response to our life's purpose or calling.
2. CHANGE as CHOICE: Change as Choice occurs when change is initiated because there is a perceived benefit of some sort.
3. CHANGE as CATAPULT: Change as Catapult occurs when life and/or situations catapult or force us into change.

> There has never been and never will be another you. You have a purpose — a very special gift that only you can bring to the world.
>
> –Marie Forleo

CHANGE AS CALLING

Change as Calling is change in pursuit of your purpose, deep longing or Spiritual or Divine summons. I have always been drawn to knowledge and I have been particularly curious for as long as I can remember. I was a child when I wrote my first little book. I wrote about all the things I wanted to do when I grew up. I wanted to be a doctor, a lawyer and a writer, but most of all, I wanted to be a teacher. I was inspired by the teachers who have served as great mentors in my life. Teaching is the work I've always longed to do; it just looks a little different than the traditional classroom setting.

My life's work is centered around some of what you will experience in this book. I am called to teach, speak, facilitate, learn, grow, and share in ways that create positive change in accordance with my values. There have been times in my life when I realized some of the work I elected to do was not (or no longer aligned) with my values, or in some cases, it was in complete contradiction to my values. Because of this awareness, I knew something had to change. As it relates to Change as Calling, I had to see teaching differently. I had to be willing to see my life's work from a broader perspective. I had to think outside of the box and reimagine the ways I could serve as a teacher, for example: facilitating classes for learners in correctional settings, on cruise ships, on sofas in the corner of school libraries, and in fancy, corporate training rooms. I had to be willing to do things differently, and you will too. Knowing you have a calling bears with it a Divine responsibility, and it is your right to answer and respond to your calling and make the changes necessary to create a safe space for you to walk in it.

> Every single choice we make is either going to enhance the spirit or drain it. Every day, we're either giving ourselves power or taking it away.
>
> –Caroline Myss

CHANGE AS CHOICE

Change as Choice is a little different than being called to change but sometimes they are interconnected. Becoming aware and/or accepting our calling often propels us to make other choices that enable us to be more effective and credible in executing our calling. When I realized my calling as a teacher/trainer, I knew I needed to work on my competencies. In my case, that meant going to school. I chose to create positive change in that area by completing my bachelor's, master's and doctorate degrees and obtaining ongoing professional certification in my field.

When I got serious about my business, I realized I had many of the technical skills required for my career, but I knew very little about what it took to run a successful business. I then chose to create positive change in that area and invest in a business development program.

When I visited the Caribbean for the first time, its beauty swept me off my feet. This feeling was so powerful that I made the commitment to experience living there. I chose to create and seek out opportunities to work and live in the Caribbean. It took me four years to make my dream a reality, but trust me when I tell you commitment and intention are pure magic when it comes to change. ⦿

> All changes, even the most longed for, have their melancholy; for what we leave behind us is a part of ourselves; we must die to one life before we can enter another.
>
> –Anatole France

CHANGE AS CATAPULT

Lastly, Change as Catapult is unexpected change, a force of nature, or otherwise beyond our control. During my last semester of college, just a month or so before graduation, I was catapulted into change by a fire in which I lost everything—well, everything that wasn't in my car. After going to seven different colleges and universities, I had decided to get serious and do whatever it took to complete my degree. I was so broke at that time in my life. I was working two or three jobs to make ends meet. I had made some very uncomfortable adjustments to put myself in a position to finish school, and then the fire happened. I spent the first twenty-four to forty-eight hours in shock, not sure what to do next or how to move forward. Then, while looking out of the balcony of my relative's home in San Francisco, I realized I could dust myself off and start all over. Perhaps the expansiveness of the beautiful bay view made me believe I could expand too. I didn't share my feelings with anyone, but somehow I knew everything would be okay. In that moment, a feeling of grace poured over me and I accepted the situation for what it was: a beautiful opportunity to begin again.

I am forever grateful for the outpouring of love and support from my family, friends, and professors without whom I don't think I could have been able to complete my final coursework and later go on to earn my graduate degrees. *Shift* happens to all of us! At some point in your life, you will be catapulted into change, whether you like it or not, and no matter how bad it seems, you can take courage through the fire and begin again.

It was just that simple, but I never said it was easy. What I offer you is this: If you are willing understand the fundamentals of change, embrace change from a position of power, and commit to changing what you can, you will change things for the better in your life. ❧

Reflections

> Your life does not get better by
> chance; it gets better by change.
>
> –Jim Rohn

In what ways are you being called to change? What do you know to be true about your life's work? What choices do you need to make to pursue your calling? How has being catapulted into change made your life better?

_____

_____

_____

_____

_____

_____

_____

_____

_____

_____

_____

_____

_____

_____

_____

_____

_____

_____

_____

_____

_____

_____

_____

_____

_____

_____

_____

_____

_____

_____

You have the power to change your life. ❦

YOUR TREASURED LIFE

> We can only be said to be alive in those moments when our hearts are conscious of our treasures.
>
> –Thornton Wilder

All the changes I've endeavored to make in my life were based on my decision to live differently. I decided many years ago that I didn't want to just exist or survive. I want to thrive and live a life I love—my treasured life. My minimum requirements for treasured living are as follows:

❖ Owning my calling and doing work I love.

❖ Living a lifestyle that is fun, flexible, filled with adventure—one that allows me to live and travel to my favorite places and do my favorite things (with my favorite people).

❖ Living and working in environments where I can thrive and I am surrounded by beauty and love.

❖ Knowing what I aspire to do in this world, holding those aspirations in my heart, and allowing them to unfold in Divine time.

❖ Being involved in healthy, loving relationships with people I appreciate, respect, and admire. My intention is to be blessed by and to be a blessing to all I encounter.

I had to get clear on what treasured living means for me and this clarity serves as a compass for positive change in my life. We must lovingly encourage one another to stand up in our calling and create bold, beautiful visions for our lives and our work. I challenge you to choose for yourself. I challenge you to put away everything you have been told you must do or be and begin to create a life you love.

Reflections

> Invent your world. Surround
> yourself with people, colors, sounds,
> and work that nourish your soul.
>
> –Susan Ariel Rainbow
> Kennedy, a/k/a SARK

What does living a treasured life mean to you? What are your requirements for a life well lived? How are your values reflected in your lifestyle? What ways of living are most important to you?

_____

_____

_____

_____

_____

_____

_____

_____

_____

_____

_____

_____

_____

_____

_____

_____

_____

_____

_____

_____

_____

_____

_____

_____

_____

_____

_____

_____

_____

Your life deserves a vision. Your work longs to
move through you out into the world. ❦

CHANGE AND THE SOUL

> Ours is not the task of fixing the entire world all at once, but of stretching out to mend the part of the world that is within our reach. One of the most calming and powerful actions you can do to intervene in a stormy world is to stand up and show your soul. Soul on deck shines like gold in dark times. The light of the soul throws sparks, can send up flares, builds signal fires.
>
> —Clarissa Pinkola Estés

I would be remiss to mention change and neglect to revere the Soul. The Soul and positive change are wonderfully intertwined. One feeds the other, and they move with grace and ease. Life always invites us to change in ways that nurture and feed our Soul. ❦

Allow your Soul to guide you along your change journey because:

- Your Soul knows **what** needs to change and why.
- Your Soul knows **when** it is best to make changes.
- Your Soul can guide you on **how** to make positive change happen in your life.

I connect to the Soul through spiritual practice,

and I also extend this practice to expand and inform my conceptualization of the Soul and change. Use the letters of the word S-O-U-L to help extend your conceptualization of the Soul:

❖ Situation—the unique place you find yourself in this space in time.

❖ Objectives—the goals you intend to achieve or obstacles you endeavor to overcome.

❖ Understanding—what you know to be true; do your best to separate the facts from fiction here.

❖ Leanings—look inside at your true nature and don't feel pressured to be someone you are not.

This expanded notion of the Soul helps me to create positive change in my life in ways that are meaningful to me. Being in step with your Soul allows you to release the overwhelm that comes from feeling like you must rush or fix things right away. There is no need to try to change things overnight. You don't have to rush. You can feel free to move at your own pace—just make sure you are inching your way towards the change you desire.

When considering ways to create positive change in your life and your world, your Soul will lead you to the areas of your life that you are empowered to impact. In these areas, you assume the position of conscious actor, whereby you assess your current reality, then choose to change in ways that are meaningful to you.

Reflections

> Your Soul—that inner quiet space—
> is yours to consult. It will always
> guide you in the right direction.
>
> –Wayne Dyer

How do you connect to your Soul? What messages are your Soul sending you about positive changes you need to make? How will you change in ways that are unique and special to your situation, objectives, understanding, and leanings?

_____

_____

_____

_____

_____

_____

_____

_____

_____

_____

_____

_____

_____

_____

_____

_____

_____

_____

_____

_____

_____

_____

_____

_____

_____

_____

_____

_____

_____

_____

_____

Positive change is a conscious act of courage. ❦

Change can be scary,
but you know what's
scarier? Allowing
fear to stop you from
growing, evolving,
and progressing.

— *Mandy Hale*

THE FIVE FOUNDATIONS OF PERSONAL POSITIVE CHANGE

> Every day is a chance to begin again. Don't focus on the failures of yesterday, start today with positive thoughts and expectations.
>
> – Catherine Pulsifer

When contemplating ways to create positive change in your life, know that you hold the power. You are infinitely powerful because there are many areas of positive change within your direct sphere of influence. You are the CCO or the Chief Change Officer of your life and creating positive change is well within your reach.

Are you ready to change but not sure where to begin? There are five areas of your life where you can begin to harness the power of positive change for yourself, and by yourself, if necessary.

♦ **New View**: Be willing to **SEE** things clearly.
♦ **New Do**: Be ready to **DO** things differently.
♦ **New Crew**: Be prepared to surround yourself with the right **PEOPLE**.

◆ **New Avenue**: Be determined to put yourself **WHERE** you really want to be.

◆ **New Source of Revenue**: Be able to create new **INCOME** streams.

These foundations of personal positive change are accessible to everyone. You can begin to change your life today from where you are now. When you decide to see things differently, do things differently, choose your relationships wisely, go where you are called and become deliberate about how you serve, you will change your life for the better.

Reflections

> Take the first step in faith. You
> don't have to see the whole
> staircase, just take the first step."
>
> – Martin Luther King Jr.

Where would you like to begin creating positive change in your life? Which facet or facets can you use today to change your life for the better?

_____

_____

_____

_____

_____

_____

_____

_____

_____

_____

_____

_____

_____

_____

_____

_____

_____

_____

_____

_____

_____

_____

_____

_____

_____

_____

_____

_____

_____

_____

_____

_____

_____

Lead the change you wish to see in your life. ▽

Every passage in this book is designed to inspire and encourage you to explore, examine, and create positive change for yourself. Bit by bit, your life can and will change for the better. The section that follows is comprised of twenty-one Jewels of Wisdom to help you take the incremental and incredible steps necessary to create positive change in your life, on your terms.

You must welcome change as the rule but not as your ruler.

—Denis Waitley

Understanding and Opportunity

Positive change invites us to raise
our awareness and broaden our
understanding of change. In
deepening our understanding, change
is demystified, and we can see it
for what it really is: an opportunity
for us to begin again. When we
are thrust into change, we have an
opportunity to acknowledge our
oneness with humanity because
no one is exempt from change.
When we choose to change for
ourselves, we enter the realm of pure
potential and begin the journey
towards all we are meant to be.

The degree of responsibility you take for your life determines how much change you can create in it.

–Celestine Chua

Change and choice go hand in hand. When we decide to change our lives for the better, we always have a choice about what we will change and how we embark on our positive change journey. We can choose to approach change in a more gentle, loving way and ease into it; or we can rip the proverbial bandage off and dive right in. Even when we are thrust into change unexpectedly or forcefully, we can choose what we will do next to embrace the new situation or create a different path altogether. Believing we don't have any options can lead us into self-imposed desperation, so we must remember we all have choices. Choosing is positive change in action! Every action has a consequence. Even when the results aren't exactly what we expect, we inch closer to our destination and we learn valuable lessons about ourselves and others. Create positive change in your life today by examining what areas in your life require change, review your available choices, then prioritize those that put you on the path towards the vision you have for your life. You have the right and power to choose. You can make choices to lead you in the direction of your ultimate goals and dreams. Let conscious choice empower you on your journey towards positive change.

Choice is a beautiful responsibility—
use it often and use it wisely.

When life calls us, that's
when we have to answer.

–Louise Hay

What is your purpose? What are you called here
to do? Many people struggle with the answers to
these questions when cues and clues are all around
us. Consider your gifts, unique talents, and abilities.
Examine the injustices you find intolerable. Listen
to the whispers you have heard time and time again
about the role you must play in our world and commit
to changing your life in ways that honor your calling.
One of the best gifts we can offer the world is to
be who we were called to be and to do what we
were called to do. Understanding our calling is the
easiest way to live a treasured life. Even when times
are challenging, you will rest with blessed assurance

that you are doing your work—the work for which you were Divinely designed. What could be greater than this?

Own your calling and create
positive change in your life.

All great changes are
preceded by chaos.

–Deepak Chopra

Sometimes we hear the whisper, but we refuse to change. Perhaps we've said yes only to realize we really should have said no and then we suffer the consequences of refusing a new choice. Other times we find ourselves so comfortable with discomfort, we decide to settle for the known versus pursuing the new. But here's the thing: when it is time to change and you choose not to, you might be catapulted into change. This happened to me just a month before my graduation from college, when I was catapulted due to a fire, and I was forced to begin again. Later I was catapulted out of an unsatisfying career due to personal illness. My diagnosis forced me to take better care of my health. When it became clear my lifestyle and way of working were in contradiction to healthy living, I resigned and relocated to the West Coast. I've been thrust off my comfort throne by these and many, many other life-altering situations. Maybe your catapult is a family health challenge, finances or a toxic relationship. Maybe it is being laid off from work, retirement, divorce or losing someone you love. Whatever the case may be, you are equipped. You can make it through by taking a little time to think about how you want to use this moment to begin again. Beauty often emerges out of chaos, so be on the lookout for new blessings life has in store.

Unexpected change often holds
unexpected blessings.

Reflections

> Clinging to the past is the problem.
> Embracing change is the answer.
>
> —Gloria Steinem

I now understand that change is:

_____

_____

_____

_____

_____

_____

_____

_____

_____

_____

_____

_____

_____

_____

_____

When your clarity
meets your conviction
and you apply action
to the equation,
your world will
begin to transform
before your eyes.

–Lisa Nichols

Clarity and Openness

Your positive change journey requires cultivation of a clear and open mind. Of critical importance is the ability to see things clearly so that you can examine your thoughts and ensure they are fertile ground in which your seeds of change can grow. When you have doubts, questions or fears, you can call in sacred wisdom, your deepest internal knowing, to receive the answers you need to proceed.

I now know that nothing in my
life will change until I change the
way I see my life and myself.

–Iyanla Vanzant

Cultivating a mindset conducive to positive change is about seeing things clearly. Sometimes it is about seeing the truth for yourself versus through the lens of others or accepting the truth versus all of the many stories you've been told. Other times it involves releasing outdated ways of thinking. Seeing for yourself improves your understanding. You may uncover completely new ways of looking at things or decide to rest in tradition. There could also be a new realization of value. Most of all, a new view involves a closer examination of your current state, or where you are now, so you can begin to envision where you intend to be.

When faced with a challenge such as job loss, create positive change by taking some time to examine the situation through the lens of radical optimism. For example, being downsized or laid off from your job can be viewed as a chance to focus on self-care or to reinvent your career. A bad breakup may provide an opportunity to develop yourself and deepen your connections to friends and loved ones. If your behavior or the behavior of others involved was less than ideal, refuse to allow criticism and negativity to cloud your view. Instead, imagine yourself and others behaving in ways that honor and support all involved. Allow yourself to imagine all the possible positive outcomes of a situation and then imagine yourself living in those possibilities. See the blessings, wonder, and potential positive change holds.

Seeing things clearly, for yourself, is the
first step to creating positive change.

We can't become what we need to
be by remaining what we are.

–Oprah Winfrey

What are the ties that bind you from experiencing peace and joy? What arrangements, agreements or relationships have you mentally or emotionally held captive? Freedom is a state of mind. Freedom is also a choice. Freedom involves a critical examination of all you hold dear and deciding what is in the way of you living your treasured life. You are the only one who can set yourself free from disruptive habits. Sure, you may have support along the way, but you are the one who ultimately holds the responsibility and power of ensuring your words, actions, interactions, and associations are true reflections of how you intend to be in the world. If you do not feel good about your current state, create positive change by giving yourself permission to free yourself, bit by bit. If you are unhappy with your current living arrangement, consider setting thirty-, sixty- or ninety-day goals to change things for the better or ease yourself out. If you are in an abusive personal or professional relationship, even if it is one you prayed for, give yourself permission to change your mind and plan your exit strategy. If goal setting isn't your thing, simply take one small step today and prepare yourself to take another one every week or every month until you are free. If you are not sure where to begin, give yourself permission to seek counsel within and from others and remain open to seeing situations from different perspectives. Do something differently to change your life for the better. You'll thank yourself later.

Stand in your power to boldly and
bravely create a life you love.

The Divine Spirit within protects,
but it doesn't interfere. It warns,
but it doesn't intrude. It guides,
but it doesn't impose. It waits
for you…but it is patient.

–Sonia Choquette

Have you ever found yourself searching feverishly for something only to realize the thing you were searching for is well within your reach, but you were not even aware it existed? So often, we overexert ourselves trying to find solutions to our problems. We run up and down searching high and low, forcing solutions onto perceived problems until we have run ourselves ragged only to find that what we were missing was available to us all along. We sped by it and were unable to see it. We were blind to the blessings right before us. I cannot count the number of times I have looked and looked for an answer and it was there all the time, hidden just behind an intense brainstorming session or muted due to all of the noise and conversations in my head. Make time today to take a few deep breaths, close your eyes and mouth, and open your ears and heart. Listen for and to your inner wisdom. It will surely guide you to all the solutions you seek.

Taking time to listen to our inner guide for wisdom is important to discovering and uncovering our life's questions. Lead yourself by availing yourself to yourself.

Reflections

> Do not compare, do not measure.
> No other way is like yours. All other
> ways deceive and tempt you. You
> must fulfill the way that is in you.
>
> –Carl Jung

It is important for me to change:

_____

_____

_____

_____

_____

_____

_____

_____

_____

_____

_____

Each time a door
closes, the rest of the
world opens up.

—Parker J. Palmer

Faith and Fate

Positive change is change that trusts, acknowledges, and accepts the impact of Divine Order. We must approach change with faithfulness, fatefulness, and with the understanding that Divide Order is ever present and prevalent. Whether we are granted favor or given rejection, we must rest assured everything is working out for our best and highest good. All our efforts are anchored in faith and trust in our Source.

Often we look so long at the closed
door that we do not see the one
that has been opened for us.

–Helen Keller

Have you ever wanted something...I mean REALLY wanted to manifest something in your life so badly you started to force your will onto people and situations? When you hold a desire deeply in your intentions and you see an opening—even if it's just big enough to get your toes underneath—there is often an inclination to pry it open instead of allowing opportunity to welcome you in. There is an unfathomable beauty in way openings—when all of your preparation and investment finally meet opportunity face-to-face. Consider taking a few steps then allowing the Universe to ease you forward in the direction of your dreams. When I first started my consulting business, I knew I wanted to do work I loved and have more freedom and income, but I wasn't exactly clear on how make it happen. I just inched forward, doing my best, while learning from people who had achieved success in similar fields and prayed. I inched forward and secured a business name, developed my mission, vision and values, opened a business checking account, and prayed. Shortly thereafter, I was presented with an opportunity to execute my first contract with more pay and much more flexibility than I had in my full-time corporate role.

When you pace yourself and pray, doors open for you that remain locked for others. Provision flows from unexpected sources. Spirit tempers your actions and takes the wheel. Want to know the difference between a no and a not-right-now? See the opportunities that avail themselves to you and have the courage to receive them, ready or not. After all, there is rarely a better time than when the Universe has orchestrated the opening on your behalf.

When doors open toward the intentions of your heart, walk boldly and courageously in.

Nothing in life has happened to
you. It's happened for you. Every
disappointment. Every wrong.
Even every closed door has helped
make you into who you are.

–Joel Osteen

Have you ever been waiting for that big call
with your big break that never comes? How about
an acceptance letter or long anticipated invitation
you have been waiting patiently to receive? Maybe
it's the "thanks but no thanks" from a prospective
employer or the unreciprocated advance of a suitor
or even an unreturned call from a loved one when
you really thought you needed it. Despite all of
your hope and effort, you realize that door is closed,

for now at least. There is much to be said about way closing. There are times in life when doors swing wide open for us, inviting us in with a warm welcome and there are other times when the door slams shut without a fond farewell. There have been times I've been denied opportunities that I felt should have been mine and later realized they weren't for me at all. Think of all the ways we force and demand our way, only to find out it wasn't what we really wanted or what we imaged it would be. We must use care in our prayers because we just may get what we pray for.

When you ask for Spirit's intervention in your life and you do what you should do and the door remains closed, be grateful and know there is something better in store. You may find yourself looking back in gratitude at the locked door.

Do your best and leave the rest. See
way closing as a blessing.

In every moment, the Universe is whispering to you. You're constantly surrounded by signs, coincidences, and synchronicities, all aimed at propelling you in the direction of your destiny.

–Denise Linn

Have you ever summoned the courage to make a decision and later questioned whether it was the right one? I don't know about you, but I have yet to make a decision that didn't have an accompanying sign, signal or gentle nudge from my emotional guidance system. While traveling along your soulful change journey, listen to what you hear around you. Look out for the signs and signals confirming you are headed in the right direction. Feel the messages your body and heart are telling you about your intentions. Decipher the difference between foreboding and fear. If you feel clear warning signs, obey them and be grateful because to be forewarned is to be forearmed. If you determine you are experiencing fear, feel your way through it and do it anyway.

Create positive change for yourself by recognizing and honoring signs from the Divine.

Reflections

> When your failures surround
> you and all the open doors have
> closed, look up. There's a door
> that never closes, a way, when all
> the other ways have failed you.
>
> –Yasmin Mogahed

I know I am on the right path because:

_____

_____

_____

_____

_____

_____

_____

_____

_____

_____

_____

_____

_____

God grant me the
serenity to accept
the things I cannot
change, the courage
to change the things I
can, and the wisdom
to know the difference.

–Reinhold Niebuhr

Decisiveness and Action

Your positive change journey
continues with a commitment
to action. Your actions can be
incremental or incredible, gradual
or grandiose. What you do and
how you do it is entirely up to you,
but you must decide to do things
differently. Based on your decisions,
be prepared to invest the time and
resources necessary to enable you
to reach your desired outcome.

If you want something different,
you are going to have to do
something different.

–Jack Canfield

After getting a clear picture of where you are, you must commit to do things differently to create the changes you wish to have in your life. This involves a commitment to doing what you *can* do to change things for the better. For a gentler approach to change, think of *can* in terms of the following:

C – Capacity: Be honest about your bandwidth. What are you honestly capable of doing at this moment in time in your life? No judgment. No comparison. You are enough.

A – Ability: Be honest about your abilities. Passion is not the same as preparation. Do what it takes to position yourself for the success you want in life and the changes you want to create.

N – Nature: Be yourself. Lead with the things that come naturally for you. This is where your God-given talents and strengths come into play. Do what it takes to develop your natural gifts and use them to create positive change for yourself and others.

Owning what you *can* do positions you to make decisions and take concrete actions to create positive changes in your life, on your own terms.

Nothing is so exhausting as
indecision, and nothing is so futile.

–Bertrand Russell

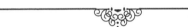

Are you willing to make positive changes in your life but not sure where to begin? Maybe you've been dreaming about starting a new business venture. Perhaps you want to publish your first book or write a screenplay. What challenges do you dare to surmount? Is there something or someone standing between you and your treasured life? If so, decide to do something about it. No more excuses. No more buts, what ifs, if onlys... The most empowering thing you can do to create positive change in your life today is to decide to change. Determine where you want to go. Decide a good place to begin. There is no need to concern yourself with the size of the decision because remember: small changes can have significant results.

Take an incremental or incredible step
in the direction of your dreams.

It's never a waste of time or money
to invest in yourself, no matter the
source. True wealth begins inwards
and emits its light outward into
everything else, including the people
you surround yourself with.

–will.i.am

What knowledge, skills or support do you need
to set yourself up for success? Are you willing to
invest in yourself to get what you say you want in
life? I realized many years ago the value of investing
in myself. Through my formal education, I was
able to use new skills and knowledge to advance
my career and take on leadership roles. I have
invested in business development coaching to help
grow and expand my business. I've also invested

in my personal development by attending retreats and seminars focusing on health, wellness, and spiritual practice. I remain committed to investing my time, money, heart, and soul into creating an environment for personal and professional success. Create positive change in your life today by choosing to sow your dreams. Pick up books by subject matter experts in your field. Spend time listening to your favorite podcasts and watching online videos. Download apps to help extend your mindfulness practice and fitness regimen. Remember: You are a worthy investment! Never underestimate the value of investing in yourself and never doubt your worthiness. Your dreams deserve your time, money, energy, and love to grow and blossom into reality.

Investing in yourself positions you for success.

Reflections

> The best investment you
> can make is in yourself.
>
> –Warren Buffett

I invest in myself by:

_____

_____

_____

_____

_____

_____

_____

_____

_____

_____

_____

_____

_____

_____

_____

_____

Maintaining a
complicated life
is a great way to
avoid changing it.

–Elaine St. James

Permission and Diligence

Positive change is change with the explicit intention of making things better. In our attempts to make things better, it is important to establish personal sanctions. Personal sanctions are sacred agreements we make with ourselves that must be treated with deep reverence. There will be things you will choose not to do, so that you can do what you must. This often involves giving yourself permission to say no, asking for help, and lightening your load a bit in support of a gentler approach to change.

The change we are looking for is always a change within ourselves. And the change will come. I've noticed that as long as I'm willing to be different, something or someone arrives to show me how.

–Marianne Williamson

It is becoming increasingly more difficult to ask for help. We are often overwhelmed. The people around us are often overwhelmed as well, and we would never want to be a burden. Sometimes we fear that asking for help makes us vulnerable and exposes the fact that there are things we simply do not know. I want you to know that it is okay. We are not supposed to know everything. It is impossible to know everything. That is one of the reasons we are here—to share knowledge by lending a helping hand to those in need and extending our hands when we need assistance. The influx of technology coupled with increased professional and personal demands compels us to think on our feet and try to find the answers, all of them, and fast! Unfortunately this can lead to information overload and create barriers to positive change. There are times when we don't know, and you know what—we don't need to know. Omniscience is reserved for the Divine. This is when we must rest in wisdom and allow Spirit to flow help our way.

Asking for assistance is a critical component
of self-mastery and positive change.

My goal is no longer to get more
done, but rather to have less to do.

–Francine Jay

Overcommitment. What is at the core of
committing ourselves beyond what is sane or
healthy? Is it an attempt to be our best or be
responsible? Maybe we want to ensure we are seen
as professional, dependable or reliable. What I know
for sure is this: underneath the veil of overdoing is a
little or a lot of fear and insecurity. We are afraid to
say no, even when we know we should. We sincerely
don't want to disappoint others, especially those
closest to us. The pandemic of placing unrealistic
expectations on ourselves and on others is a form of
abuse and the antithesis of positive change. What
would happen if we chose to say no? What would

happen if we chose ourselves and our families first? Overcommitting is one of the easiest ways to separate ourselves from the Source. It is difficult to serve others when our fatigue makes us a fraction of ourselves. Sometimes saying no to others is the only way to say yes to ourselves. We *can* get off the drain train at the next stop.

Knowing when to say no and having the courage to do so clears a path for positive change.

When you're overwhelmed,
tired or stressed,
the solution is almost always … less
Get rid of something.
Lots of somethings.

–Courtney Carver

Look around your home. Examine your life. Are there any items that have served you well but are no longer useful or practical? Is there anything that definitely needs to be released or tossed out? All too often we keep items around that have served us well but are no longer useful. In fact, they are weighing us down. I have personally contributed to the billion-dollar self-storage industry to keep items "just in case." It has taken me years to discover I don't need much to be happy. Bless someone today by donating items to charity or simply sharing with someone in need. Make a commitment to free your space and yourself from excess because less is often so much more.

Lightening your load can make it easier to lead yourself and make space for positive change.

Reflections

> The day she let go of the things that were weighing her down, was the day she began to shine the brightest.
>
> –Katrina Mayer

I create positive change by releasing:

_____

_____

_____

_____

_____

_____

_____

_____

_____

_____

_____

_____

_____

_____

When we choose to
love, we choose to
move against fear,
against alienation and
separation. The choice
to love is a choice
to connect, to find
ourselves in the other.

–*Bell Hooks*

Relating and Connections

Positive change includes being more intentional in our relations. Sometimes we have a desire to deepen our existing relationships. Other times we choose to create new connections. The journey towards positive change compels us to take a close, loving look at the people we have called into our lives. It also asks us to give thoughtful consideration of who we are in relationship with and how we relate to others.

Align yourself with people that you can learn from, people who want more out of life, people who are stretching and searching and seeking some higher ground in life.

–Les Brown

You are at the center of positive change in your life, but change rarely happens in isolation. As your life begins to change, these changes may have an impact on your relationships. As we grow, we hope others around us will accept our changes and grow along with us. This is not always the case. It may be necessary to find a new crew—one with whom you can thrive. In business relationships, be prepared to expand your connections to include the mentors, partners, and colleagues that offer value-for-value relationships because you deserve it. In personal relationships, love your family and partners where they are. The closer the relationship, the greater the impact your changes may have on your loved ones. The stronger the relationship, the greater the chance it has of surviving the storms change can bring. When the dust settles, you'll be greater and stronger together. If you know staying together is not possible, prepare to gently release those relationships that are fair-weather, destructive, shallow or stagnant. Their time has come to an end. Open yourself to better relationships because you deserve more. You alone are responsible and accountable for changing your life for the better, but you do not have to do it alone.

Surrounding yourself with great people allows you to elevate yourself and be the best you can be.

The great benefit of slowing down is reclaiming the time and tranquility to make meaningful connections—with people, with culture, with work, with nature, with our own bodies and minds.

–Carl Honoré

What comes to mind when you consider closeness? We have the ability to communicate at the speed of light, but do our communications convey the quality of the connection? We are connected to the internet, our cell phones and tablets, but are we connected to Spirit, our Soul yearnings and those we hold dear? Sure, there are times when we all must disconnect and hide ourselves from world. Yet there is no denying: we need one another. Nothing can take the place of loving human interactions. We must find a way to connect with ourselves and those we hold dear. Illness and loss have a way of reminding us to take a moment to reconnect and focus on the important things in life. We can make a conscious, deliberate choice to check ourselves instead our emails. We can do our best to connect with ourselves and our family and friends in ways that build and sustain relationships. I don't mean approaching connections like something on a to-do list, nor do I mean giving too much of ourselves to others and feeling drained. We can find a happy medium—one that loves and nurtures and enables relationships to last a lifetime.

Harnessing the ability to connect is essential for relationships of any sort. We cannot thrive as a community without it.

We don't need to explain our
love. We only need to show it.

–Paulo Coelho

How does your love show? Is it bright, sunny and vivacious? Is it pensive, tentative or reserved? And how do you know? The people we show love to and share love with are often beautiful reflections of the way we make meaning of love. When we love too hard, sometimes we injure ourselves or those around us. When we love too strong, sometimes we break bonds instead of mending them. Let's try a little tenderness. How about some soft love—love that nurtures and soothes and gives others a soft place to land. Or maybe a little slow love—a love that is patient, kind, and makes one feel at ease. There are beautiful ways to show our love. If you're not sure what they are just ask your loved ones how your love shows and how you can love them better. Be appreciative of their responses. Living well and loving well are essential for treasured living so let your love flow and grow.

Appreciation opens the doors of
love and positive change.

Reflections

> Always do your best. Your best is going to change from moment to moment; it will be different when you are healthy as opposed to sick. Under any circumstance, simply do your best, and you will avoid self-judgment, self-abuse and regret.
>
> –don Miguel Ruiz

I deepen and nurture my relationships by:

_____

_____

_____

_____

_____

_____

_____

_____

_____

_____

_____

_____

_____

When you are a young person, you are like a young creek, and you meet many rocks, many obstacles and difficulties on your way. You hurry to get past these obstacles and get to the ocean. But as the creek moves down through the fields, it becomes larger and calmer and it can enjoy the reflection of the sky. It's wonderful. You will arrive at the sea anyway so enjoy the journey. Enjoy the sunshine, the sunset, the moon, the birds, the trees, and the many beauties along the way. Taste every moment of your daily life.

– *Thich Nhat Hanh*

Detours and Sojourns

Your positive change journey will inevitably involve a detour or two. You could choose to move in a different direction. You could be called to a new location. You might realize change takes a little more time than you anticipated. You will likely be nudged outside of your comfort zones. Adopting a more loving approach to change includes seeing change as a beautiful adventure—filled with highs and lows—an adventure you can choose to enjoy.

The Spirit calls me, and I must go.

–Sojourner Truth

Some people can thrive at home. Others must travel the world to become world class. I believe it is natural to want to rest in the soothing comfort and familiarity of home. I must admit, sometimes my heart breaks when I know I must leave my family and friends behind and offer my work to the world. Despite the heartbreak, I remain determined. Despite the discomfort, the truth remains: so many of my blessings have been tied to distant journeys and new adventures. Sometimes it is necessary, even critical, to leave the nest to soar. Our greatest thought leaders and freedom fighters had to get out into the world to pursue their dreams, be who they were meant to be, and share their gifts. Sometimes we must leave to live. Leaving comfort behind, even temporarily, requires determination. The ability to manage temporary discomfort is a form of self-mastery. This separates the pretenders from the contenders in the change game.

Let your determination propel you to a fabulous new destination filled with hope and aspiration. It is time to stop living in your head and get out there to live and love your life.

Life begins at the end of your comfort zone. So if you're feeling uncomfortable right now, know that the change taking place in your life is a beginning, not an ending.

–Neale Donald Walsch

Those who know me know I'm all about a sweet adventure and I dance to the beat of my own drum. I know I am not alone. Conscious change acknowledges we are all on our own paths. Today, I own my path, and I know my positive change journey will have highs and lows. Acknowledging this truth gives me peace and encourages me to continue. Our path in life might look completely different than that of our parents, siblings or partners —even the people in our community and our closest friends.

Perhaps you've chosen to take the high road. What if you are called to go off the beaten path to take the road less traveled? Your road to positive change and treasured living might get a little uncomfortable, but there is no need to give up. Adjust if you must, but don't give up. You may have to leave your comfort zone to become more comfortable than you have ever imagined.

Venture beyond your comfort zones
and live your treasured life.

Hello Traveler,
As you make your way along life's
tumultuous highways, it's important
to note that you should always carry
a map, have plenty of fuel in the
tank, and take frequent rest stops.

–Octavia Spencer

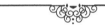

Creating positive change takes time: time to consider what you must change and how you will change things for the better, time for testing that new idea in the marketplace, time for contemplation, time for action, and time for rest. Whether starting a new job or career, launching a new business or reshaping your relationships, choosing positive change is one of the greatest gifts you can give yourself. That said, the journey towards positive change is a marathon, not a sprint. For a more soulful approach to positive change, decide to enjoy yourself along the way. In pursuit of positive change, we sometimes miss the beauty that already exists in our lives. Know you are on a journey and take time to enjoy it. Be patient with yourself and kind to those around you. Give yourself a special treat as a reward for your progress. You have so much to be grateful for and so much good in store. Remember to take good care of yourself and find joy along the way.

Choose to enjoy yourself on your
journey towards change.

Reflections

> Take pride in how far you've come.
> Have faith in how far you can go.
> But don't forget to enjoy the journey.
>
> –Michael Josephson

On my journey towards positive change, I allow myself time to:

_____

_____

_____

_____

_____

_____

_____

_____

_____

_____

_____

ABOUT THE AUTHOR

Most of us have a clear idea of what needs to change in our lives for us to be the happy, joyful and fulfilled individuals we were born and created to be. Whether the change you're seeking is a change in income, relationships or career, the question isn't what you want, it's how you're going to get it. That's where Dr. Sheree comes in.

Dr. Sheree has served learners and developed leaders in the hotel industry, healthcare institutions, Fortune 500 corporations, correctional education facilities and traditional academic settings. She is a motivational speaker, transformational facilitator, leadership coach and positive change catalyst whose work is grounded in a strengths-based philosophy of searching for the best in individuals and organizations. She is the owner of Sheree Sekou Consulting, a boutique learning and development firm, host of the What a Difference a Change Makes podcast, and founder of Your Treasured Life, a leadership and lifestyle brand dedicated to the people, places and things that inspire positive change. She believes that the power to change your life is in your hands and she's developed transformational coaching and learning programs that will help you get where you're going without the guesswork.

Dr. Sheree's expertise comes not only from her education and work experience, but from a full life of seeking and courageously leaping forward to a treasured life. She "feels the fear and does it anyway", and by leading through example, she helps her clients do the same. An avid business and personal traveler, Dr. Sheree has journeyed to six of the seven continents, and she currently resides in the Houston area and the U.S. Virgin Islands with her hubby. She considers herself a lifelong student of spirituality, personal empowerment and self-mastery.

To learn more about Dr. Sheree's products and services, go to www.shereesekouconsulting.com